Facts About the Roseate Spoonbill

By Lisa Strattin

© 2016 Lisa Strattin

Facts for Kids Picture Books by Lisa Strattin

Sign Up for New Release Emails Here

http://lisastrattin.com/subscribe-here

Join the KidCrafts Monthly Program Here

http://KidCraftsByLisa.com

## Table of Contents

# INTRODUCTION

The Roseate Spoonbill is both beautiful and ugly at the same time. They have beautiful colored feathers on their bodies – pink, rose, orange, white, and black. But then they have an ugly bald head and a funny-looking beak too!

This is a large wading bird living in groups called colonies. Most often you can find them around salt water lagoons or fresh water wetlands. As a species, they were almost totally eliminated by the early 20th century, but their populations have increased steadily since then.

## CHARACTERISTICS

Adults and juvenile birds spend much of their time wading through shallow water. They will put their heads down and begin to swing from side to side, poking around with their long beaks to find something tasty to eat. They are active during the daytime. At night they will roost in nearby trees.

## APPEARANCE

At first these birds may remind you of the flamingo which is another large and pink colored wading bird. But flamingos and spoonbills are not the same species. The head of the spoonbill is bald and a grey-green color. It has red eyes and a long grey beak which looks like a flat spoon at the end. There are white, pink and dark pink (rose) colored feathers on its body and wings. The tail is orange. It stands on long skinny legs with knees that bend backwards instead of forwards. Juvenile birds have light pink feathers instead of all the colors that you see in the adults.

11

# LIFE STAGES

Life begins when the mother lays eggs in a nest. There can be 2 – 5 eggs laid at the same time. Both mother and father bird take turns sitting on their eggs. A few weeks later, the babies, called chicks, will break out of the eggs. Both parents will feed their chicks. The chicks stay in the nest until they grow bigger, lose their soft baby down and develop feathers. About two months later they become juveniles and can fly and leave the nest. They learn how to forage for food by watching their parents and other adult birds. Once they lose the light pink feathers and develop all the adult feather colors, they become adults.

## LIFE SPAN

In the wild this bird can live to be 10 years old.

## SIZE

This is a big bird. It stands about 2 and 1/2 feet tall. The males are bigger than the females.

# HABITAT

You can find these birds along the coast of southeastern United States from Texas all the way to Florida. Their range extends from the USA south to include Central America and much of South America. They live by lagoons, mangrove bays, lakes, and marshes. These habitats can be freshwater, salt water, or brackish water which is a mixture of both fresh and salt water.

## DIET

They like to eat small crustaceans such as shrimp and crayfish. Their diet also includes slugs, snails, and some insects.

# FRIENDS AND ENEMIES

Roseate Spoonbills get along with other wading birds found in their environments. Examples of other wading birds would be herons, ibises, cormorants, and ducks.

Alligators, crocodiles, panthers, and jaguars are their main predators. Another enemy is the anaconda – a huge snake that lives in South America. This snake can wrap its body around the bird's body and squeeze it to death. Raccoons, river otters, and small tree snakes won't attack the adult birds but will steal their eggs or newborn chicks for a meal.

The problem facing these birds today is the loss of their habitats due to water pollution or draining of swamps by humans for new housing construction.

# SUITABILITY AS PETS

The Roseate Spoonbill is not suitable as a pet. They need to live with their own kind and to find mates for reproduction. It is way too big for a cage and would not sleep with you in your bed. Because it would feel trapped, the bird would try to escape. It could fly into furniture or windows and break things. It might even injure itself or you or someone else in your house as it fights to get out. This is not a good idea.

It is much better to leave these birds alone to live in the wild where they belong. If you like nature and bird watching, there are organizations and clubs for people like you who have these interests

35

**Please leave me a review here:**

*http://lisastrattin.com/Review-Vol-164*

**For more Kindle Downloads Visit Lisa Strattin Author Page on Amazon Author Central**

*http://amazon.com/author/lisastrattin*

**To see upcoming titles, visit my website at LisaStrattin.com – all books available on kindle!**

*http://lisastrattin.com*

# SPOONBILL PUZZLE

You can get one by copying and pasting
this link into your browser:
http://lisastrattin.com/SpoonbillPuzzle

37

# KIDCRAFTS MONTHLY
# SUBSCRIPTION PROGRAM

**Receive a Box of Crafts and a Lisa
Strattin Full Color Paperback Book Each
Month in Your Mailbox!**

Get yours by copying and pasting this link
into your browser

http://KidCraftsByLisa.com

Made in the USA
Middletown, DE
03 July 2018